COUNT YOUR

Blessings

*Received Scott &
from Dawn Caitie Dec: 2013*

© 2012 by Barbour Publishing, Inc.

Written and compiled by MariLee Parrish.

Print ISBN 978-1-61626-825-1

eBook Editions:
Adobe Digital Edition (.epub) 978-1-60742-004-0
Kindle and MobiPocket Edition (.prc) 978-1-60742-025-5

Cover and interior design: Kirk DouPonce, DogEared Design

Published by Barbour Publishing, Inc., P.O. Box 719, Uhrichsville, Ohio 44683, www.barbourbooks.com

Our mission is to publish and distribute inspirational products offering exceptional value and biblical encouragement to the masses.

 Member of the
Evangelical Christian
Publishers Association

Printed in the United States of America.

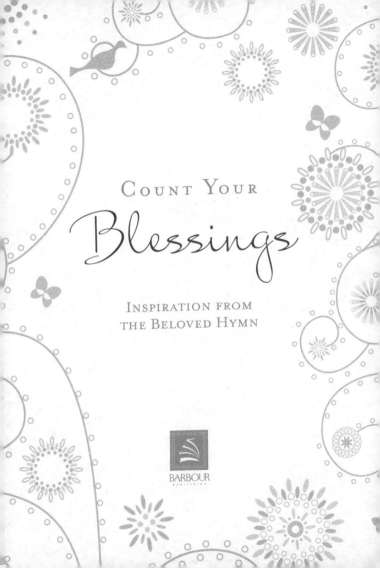

Count Your
Blessings

INSPIRATION FROM
THE BELOVED HYMN

BARBOUR

Contents

Count Your Blessings 6

Name Them One by One 9

Finding Encouragement 21

Blessings in Burdens... 33

Simple Joys 45

A Song in My Heart 57

Love: the Greatest Blessing................................. 69

He Keeps His Promises....................................... 83

Simple, Everyday Blessings 97

An Eternal Reward... 109

Blessed Freedom in Christ 123

He's in Control 135

Comfort for Today 147

Cultivating a Thankful Heart 159

Being a Blessing to Others 171

And It Will Surprise You What the Lord Has Done ... 183

Count Your Blessings

When upon life's billows you are tempest-tossed,
When you are discouraged, thinking all is lost,
Count your many blessings, name them one by one,
And it will surprise you what the Lord hath done.

CHORUS
Count your blessings, name them one by one,
Count your blessings, see what God hath done!
Count your blessings, name them one by one,
And it will surprise you what the Lord hath done.

Are you ever burdened with a load of care?
Does the cross seem heavy you are called to bear?
Count your many blessings, every doubt will fly,
And you will keep singing as the days go by.

When you look at others with their lands and gold,
Think that Christ has promised you
   His wealth untold;
Count your many blessings—wealth can never buy
Your reward in heaven, nor your home on high.

So, amid the conflict whether great or small,
Do not be disheartened, God is over all;
Count your many blessings, angels will attend,
Help and comfort give you to your journey's end.

Johnson Oatman Jr. (1897)

Name Them
One by One

Return to your rest,
my soul, for the LORD
has been good to you.
For you, LORD,
have delivered me
from death,
my eyes from tears,
my feet from stumbling.

PSALM 116:7–8 NIV

Counting our blessings can transform our outlook on life. When life is overwhelming and out of control, we can rest. We can trust the God who has been faithful in the past, to be faithful now and in all the days to come. God has blessed us abundantly! He has rescued us from death, from despair, and from humiliation. Sit down and count all the ways God has blessed you. Don't just go over them in your mind, take the time to write them down! Then when you are tempted to stress over life issues again (and those days are sure to come), you can look back at your list of blessings and remember all the ways God has been faithful to you. The Bible tells us God is the same yesterday, today, and forever (Hebrews 13:8). Relax in that truth and allow God to transform your mind-set into one of thankfulness, blessing, and peace.

Great is Thy faithfulness!
Great is Thy faithfulness!
Morning by morning new mercies I see;
All I have needed Thy hand hath provided—
Great is Thy faithfulness, Lord, unto me!

THOMAS O. CHISHOLM

Reflect upon your present blessings
of which every man has many—
not on your past misfortunes,
of which all men have some.

CHARLES DICKENS

Add to your joy by
counting your blessings.

UNKNOWN

*Jesus Christ is the same yesterday
and today and forever.*
HEBREWS 13:8 NIV

*For the word of the LORD is right and true;
he is faithful in all he does.*
PSALM 33:4 NIV

*From his abundance we have all received
one gracious blessing after another.
For the law was given through Moses,
but God's unfailing love and faithfulness
came through Jesus Christ.*
JOHN 1:16–17 NLT

Gratitude is the homage of the heart,
rendered to God for His goodness.
NATHANIEL PARKER WILLIS

Resolve to see the world on the sunny side,
and you have almost won
the battle of life at the outset.
SIR ROGER L'ESTRANGE

Take spring when it comes, and rejoice.
Take happiness when it comes, and rejoice.
Take love when it comes, and rejoice.
CARL EWALD

I Rest in Your Truth

Heavenly Father, thank You for Your
many blessings and Your unfailing love!
Allow me to rest in the truth that You are
forever the same. In times of blessing and
in hard times, too, bring me reminders
of Your faithfulness and love. Amen.

Let all that I am praise the LORD; with my whole heart,
I will praise his holy name. Let all that I am praise the
LORD; may I never forget the good things he does for me.

PSALM 103:1–2 NLT

The faithful love of the LORD never ends!
His mercies never cease. Great is his faithfulness;
his mercies begin afresh each morning.

LAMENTATIONS 3:22–23 NLT

So the Word became human and
made his home among us. He was full of
unfailing love and faithfulness.
And we have seen his glory,
the glory of the Father's one and only Son.

JOHN 1:14 NLT

The word of the LORD is right and true;
he is faithful in all he does.

PSALM 33:4 NIV

But the fruit of the Spirit is love, joy, peace,
longsuffering, kindness, goodness, faithfulness.

GALATIANS 5:22 NKJV

To be cheerful under all circumstances
is to radiate faith. It is an expression of hope
and an attitude of joyful expectance.
HANNAH WHITALL SMITH

Cheerfulness is the habit
of looking at the good side of things.
W. B. ULLATHORNE

Every sunset brings the
promise of a new dawn.
JOANIE GARBORG

Great Is Your Faithfulness

Lord, I am amazed at how faithful and merciful
You are to me. Your mercies and blessings are
new each and every day. Help me to keep
my heart set on You and to remember how
faithful You have been to me in the past.
I trust You with my future. Amen.

The best things are nearest:
breath in your nostrils, light in your eyes,
flowers at your feet, duties at your hand,
the path of God just before you.
ROBERT LOUIS STEVENSON

Life is so full of meaning and purpose,
so full of beauty, beneath its covering,
that you will find earth but cloaks your heaven.
FRA GIOVANNI

The most precious things
of life are near at hand.
JOHN BURROUGHS

Finding
Encouragement

"This is my command—
be strong and courageous!
Do not be afraid or
discouraged. For the
LORD your God is with
you wherever you go."

JOSHUA 1:9 NLT

Discouragement is everywhere. Every step in the right direction is often criticized by others. Friends, family, and even well-meaning Christians can lose sight of faith and discourage us from following God's will to the fullest. It's so important to keep our eyes on Christ and concern ourselves only with what He wants for us and not what others think. Find encouragement in the One who made you and has perfect plans for your life. Going against the norm takes courage! And God promises to be with you at all times. He is your constant encourager and comforter. Allow Him to be the center of your life. . .and His peace will guard your heart and mind (Philippians 4:6–7). Now *that's* encouraging!

Do not be anxious about anything,
but in every situation, by prayer and petition,
with thanksgiving, present your requests to God.
And the peace of God, which transcends all understanding,
will guard your hearts and your minds in Christ Jesus.

PHILIPPIANS 4:6–7 NIV

So let's not get tired of doing what is good.
At just the right time we will reap a
harvest of blessing if we don't give up.

GALATIANS 6:9 NLT

"But consider the joy of those corrected by God!
Do not despise the discipline of the Almighty when you sin.
For though he wounds, he also bandages.
He strikes, but his hands also heal."

JOB 5:17–18 NLT

Satisfy us in the morning with your unfailing love,
that we may sing for joy and be glad all our days.

PSALM 90:14 NIV

To accomplish great things,
we must not only act, but also dream;
not only plan, but also believe.
ANATOLE FRANCE

I find that doing of the will of
God leaves me no time for disputing
about His plans.
GEORGE MACDONALD

When defeat comes, accept it as a signal
that your plans are not sound,
rebuild those plans, and set sail
once more toward your coveted goal.
NAPOLEON HILL

Your Perfect Plan

Jesus, You are my friend, my comfort, and my constant encourager. Help me to seek You always and not worry about what others think. Your plan for my life is perfect and full of promise. Amen.

What a Friend we have in Jesus,
All our sins and griefs to bear!
What a privilege to carry
Everything to God in prayer!
O what peace we often forfeit,
O what needless pain we bear,
All because we do not carry
Everything to God in prayer!

JOSEPH M. SCRIVEN

Many are the plans in a person's heart,
but it is the LORD's purpose that prevails.
PROVERBS 19:21 NIV

If you plan to do evil, you will be lost;
if you plan to do good, you will receive
unfailing love and faithfulness.
PROVERBS 14:22 NLT

The plans of the LORD stand firm forever,
the purposes of his heart through all generations.
PSALM 33:11 NIV

Our God, our help in ages past,
Our hope for years to come,
Our shelter from the stormy blast,
And our eternal home.

ISAAC WATTS

Every moment is full of wonder
and God is always present.

UNKNOWN

Trusting in Your Plan

Father, thank You for Your unfailing love
that brings encouragement to my soul and
gladness to my heart. You are my ever-present
help and hope. I thank You for Your guidance
and protection day after day. Although I never
know what the day will bring, You have a plan,
and I trust in You. Amen.

When we take time to notice the simple things
in life, we never lack for encouragement.
We discover we are surrounded by limitless
hope that's just wearing everyday clothes.

UNKNOWN

Today a new sun rises for me; everything
lives, everything is animated, everything
seems to speak to me of my passion,
everything invites me to cherish it.

ANNE DE LENCLOS

Blessings in
Burdens

God is our merciful Father
and the source of all comfort.
He comforts us in all our
troubles. . . . For the more
we suffer for Christ, the more
God will shower us with his
comfort through Christ.

2 CORINTHIANS 1:3–5 NLT

Are you enrolled in the School of Hard Knocks? It may feel like that at times. The Bible tells us to expect trouble (John 16:33) because we live in a broken, fallen world. Knowing hard times are coming doesn't make it much easier, but Jesus offers us His peace at all times. We mistakenly believe that peace equals carefree days and tranquility. Missionary and author J. Oswald Sanders once said that peace isn't the absence of trouble but the presence of God in the midst of trouble. The blessing of true peace gives us the ability to make it through anything knowing that God sees our progress report and is using every problem to teach us. And in turn, we can be a blessing by comforting and teaching others so that one day we will graduate with flying colors.

Blessed be Your name
On the road marked with suffering
Though there's pain in the offering
Blessed be Your name

MATT REDMAN

If God can bring blessing from the broken body
of Jesus and glory from something that's as
obscene as the cross, He can bring blessing from
my problems and my pain and my unanswered
prayer. I just have to trust Him.

ANNE GRAHAM LOTZ

"I have told you these things, so that in me you may have peace. In this world you will have trouble. But take heart! I have overcome the world."

JOHN 16:33 NIV

"Peace I leave with you; my peace I give you. I do not give to you as the world gives. Do not let your hearts be troubled and do not be afraid."

JOHN 14:27 NIV

"The LORD gave and the LORD has taken away;
may the name of the LORD be praised."
JOB 1:21 NIV

God blesses those who mourn,
for they will be comforted.
MATTHEW 5:4 NLT

Choosing Thankfulness

Lord, I choose to thank You and trust You
in the midst of these burdens. Allow me to
be a blessing to others through what You
are teaching me. When troubles come,
I never have to face them alone. Thank You
for always being with me as my refuge and
strength. When all else fails, I put my trust
in You and am never disappointed. Amen.

*Blessed is the one who perseveres under trial because,
having stood the test, that person will receive the crown of
life that the Lord has promised to those who love him.*

JAMES 1:12 NIV

Cast all your anxiety on him because he cares for you.

1 PETER 5:7 NIV

Then Jesus turned to his disciples and said, "God blesses you who are poor, for the Kingdom of God is yours. God blesses you who are hungry now, for you will be satisfied. God blesses you who weep now, for in due time you will laugh. What blessings await you when people hate you and exclude you and mock you and curse you as evil because you follow the Son of Man. When that happens, be happy! Yes, leap for joy! For a great reward awaits you in heaven."

LUKE 6:20–23 NLT

's] care for us is more watchful
and more tender than the care of
any human father could possibly be.

HANNAH WHITALL SMITH

God never built a Christian strong enough
to carry today's duties and tomorrow's
anxieties piled on top of them.

THEODORE LEDYARD CUYLER

Worry does not empty tomorrow of its sorrow.
It empties today of its strength.

CORRIE TEN BOOM

Casting My Cares

Father, these burdens seem too much for me
to bear. I cast all my anxiety and concerns onto
Your capable shoulders. Use these trials to make
me more like You. When happiness is hard
to come by, help me to learn to draw more
consistently on Your wellspring of joy. Amen.

Grace is available for each of us every day. . .
but we've got to remember to ask for it with a
grateful heart and not worry about whether
there will be enough for tomorrow.

SARAH BAN BREATHNACH

God can heal a broken heart,
but He has to have all the pieces.

UNKNOWN

Every evening I turn my worries over to God.
He's going to be up all night anyway.

MARY C. CROWLEY

Simple Joys

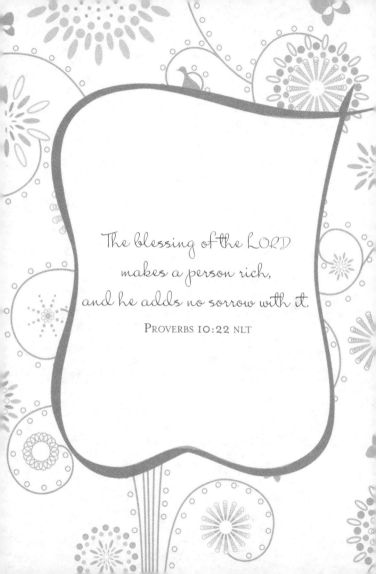

The blessing of the LORD
makes a person rich,
and he adds no sorrow with it.

PROVERBS 10:22 NLT

God's blessings—both large and small—do indeed make life rich. Instead of asking, "What's next, God?" make time to thank Him for what He's already given you. Instead of asking, "Why not me, God?" delight with your friends and family who are being blessed. Look around you and see the simple joys God has added to your world. Take joy in the children in your life, their simple faith and absolute trust in God. Enjoy God's creation all around you, the beauty in each season. Invest in the people God has placed on your path, the joy of loving and being loved. It is in these simple joys that the stuff of life is made full and we see God's blessings in everyday life. Don't take any of them for granted! As Walter Hagen, the American golfer once said: "You're only here for a short visit. Don't hurry, don't worry. And be sure to smell the flowers along the way."

Thou art giving and forgiving,
ever blessing, ever blessed,
Wellspring of the joy of living,
ocean depth of happy rest!
HENRY J. VAN DYKE

I've got the joy, joy, joy, joy
Down in my heart
Down in my heart to stay
GEORGE WILLIS COOKE

*For you make me glad by your deeds, L*ORD*;*
I sing for joy at what your hands have done.

PSALM 92:4 NIV

*Great are the works of the L*ORD*; they are pondered by all*
who delight in them. Glorious and majestic are his deeds,
and his righteousness endures forever.

PSALM 111:2–3 NIV

Jesus—Light of the world. Joy of hearts.

UNKNOWN

Joy comes, grief goes, we know not how.

JAMES RUSSELL LOWELL

When I think upon my God, my heart is so full of joy that the notes dance and leap from my pen.

FRANZ JOSEF HAYDN

I asked God for all things that I might enjoy life. He gave me life that I might enjoy all things.

UNKNOWN

Abundantly Blessed

Heavenly Father, thank You for the simple
joys of life: my health, my family, my friends.
Help me to slow down and appreciate all the
blessings in my life. You have provided me with
everything I need and have blessed me
abundantly. Help me delight in the little
gifts You bring my way every day. Amen.

As we grow in our capacities to discover
the joys that God has placed in our lives,
life becomes a glorious experience of
discovering His endless wonders.

UNKNOWN

To the children of God there stands,
behind all that changes and can change,
only one unchangeable joy. That is God.

HANNAH WHITALL SMITH

Joy is the echo of God's life within us.

JOSEPH MARMION

I have seen you in your sanctuary and gazed upon your power and glory. Your unfailing love is better than life itself; how I praise you! I will praise you as long as I live, lifting up my hands to you in prayer. You satisfy me more than the richest feast. I will praise you with songs of joy.

PSALM 63:2–5 NLT

Our God is so wonderfully good and
lovely and blessed in every way that the
mere fact of belonging to Him is enough
for an untellable fullness of joy!
HANNAH WHITALL SMITH

The mere sense of living is joy enough.
EMILY DICKINSON

A child of God should be a visible beatitude
for joy and happiness and a living
doxology for gratitude and adoration.
CHARLES H. SPURGEON

Unspeakable Joy

Lord, Your unfailing love fills me with an unspeakable joy. You have satisfied my deepest needs and continue to bring one blessing after another. Fill the reservoir of my heart to overflowing with the joy that real hope brings. Give me an eternal perspective so I never miss the simple joys You provide. Amen.

Half the joy of life is in the little things taken
on the run. . . . And everything is worth its
while if we only grasp it and its significance.

CHARLES VICTOR CHERBULIEZ

I find joy in knowing that no one can
take joy away from me. But the more
I share it, the more it multiplies.

UNKNOWN

I have a heart with room for every joy.

P. J. BAILEY

A Song
in My Heart

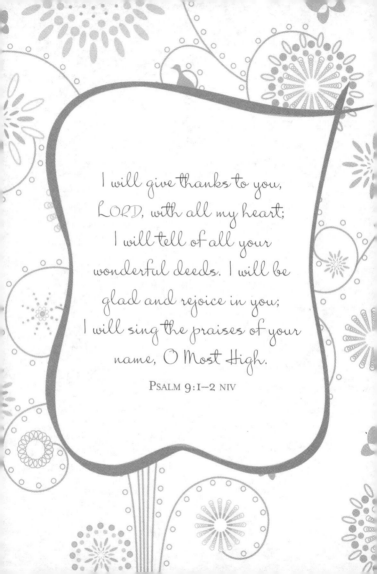

I will give thanks to you,
LORD, with all my heart;
I will tell of all your
wonderful deeds. I will be
glad and rejoice in you;
I will sing the praises of your
name, O Most High.

PSALM 9:1–2 NIV

If we are daily praising God and our hearts are full of love for Him, others cannot help but see the difference He has made in our lives. Praise and worship isn't just about singing songs at church on Sunday. It's about living my life in such a way that is pleasing to God. If we are living a life of worship, we cannot help but tell others about who He is and what He has done for us. Do you have a song in your heart? Are you filled with joy over what God has done for us? If not, then confess your lack of contentment to the Lord and ask Him to fill you to overflowing with His love and joy. Put a smile on your face and focus on how much God loves you. Living with a song in your heart will make the Father smile and can be a great witness to others wherever you go.

Worship is my response to God with all that I am
to all that He is, all that He has done, is doing,
and will do in me, through me, around me,
and in spite of me. It's not just a song. Worship
is our response with all of our lives, everything
that we've been given, to all that God is.

SHAUN GROVES

The happiest man is he who learns
from nature the lesson of worship.

RALPH WALDO EMERSON

"I will sing to the LORD, for he is highly exalted. . . .
The LORD is my strength and my defense; he has
become my salvation. He is my God, and I will praise
him, my father's God, and I will exalt him."
EXODUS 15:1–2 NIV

My heart, O God, is steadfast; I will sing
and make music with all my soul.
PSALM 108:1 NIV

For the despondent, every day brings trouble;
for the happy heart, life is a continual feast.
PROVERBS 15:15 NLT

Be merry, really merry. The life of a true
Christian should be a perpetual jubilee,
a prelude to the festivals of eternity.

THEOPHANE VENARD

The joyful birds prolong the strain,
their song with every spring renewed;
The air we breathe, and falling rain,
each softly whispers: God is good.

JOHN HAMPDEN GURNEY

Joy is the echo of God's life within us.

JOSEPH MARMION

My Song of Praise

Lord, You are the song in my heart. I worship
You with my voice, but I want to worship You
with everything else I do, too. Please show me
how to worship You with my daily life. Make me
mindful of Your great gifts, that my song may
praise Your work in my life. Amen.

God is to be praised with the voice, and the
heart should go therewith in holy exultation.

CHARLES H. SPURGEON

There's within my heart a melody
Jesus whispers sweet and low,
Fear not, I am with thee, peace, be still,
In all of life's ebb and flow.

Jesus, Jesus, Jesus,
Sweetest Name I know,
Fills my every longing,
Keeps me singing as I go.

LUTHER B. BRIDGES

Now to the King of heav'n
Your cheerful voices raise
To Him be glory giv'n, Pow'r, majesty, and praise
Wide as He reigns His name be sung by every
tongue in endless strains. Amen.
Isaac Watts and Philip Doddridge

It is not how much we have, but how
much we enjoy, that makes happiness.
Charles H. Spurgeon

It is pleasing to the dear God whenever you
rejoice or laugh from the bottom of your heart.
Martin Luther

*The LORD is my strength and shield. I trust him with
all my heart. He helps me, and my heart is filled
with joy. I burst out in songs of thanksgiving.*

PSALM 28:7 NLT

*"Blessings on the King who comes in the name of the
LORD! Peace in heaven, and glory in highest heaven!"
But some of the Pharisees among the crowd said, "Teacher,
rebuke your followers for saying things like that!"
He replied, "If they kept quiet, the stones along
the road would burst into cheers!"*

LUKE 19:38–40 NLT

My Song of Thanksgiving

Dear God, help me to live a life of worship
and to give You glory for who You are.
Let my heart be full of love for You and
allow this song in my heart to bless everyone
around me. You bless my life in many ways
every day, Father. May I receive Your blessings
with a song of thanksgiving on my lips. Amen.

Worship is the thank you
that can't be silenced.

MAX LUCADO

The most valuable thing the Psalms
do for me is to express the same delight
in God which made David dance.

C. S. LEWIS

Love:

the Greatest

Blessing

For God so loved the world that he gave his one and only Son, that whoever believes in him shall not perish but have eternal life. For God did not send his Son into the world to condemn the world, but to save the world through him.

JOHN 3:16–17 NIV

Do you know Jesus Christ as your personal
Savior? If not, you are missing out on life.
Everlasting life! Won't you take a moment
right now and surrender your life to Him?
We've all made mistakes, but the Bible tells us
that God longs to be gracious and compas-
sionate (Isaiah 30:18) and that if we accept
His gift of salvation, we can be with Him for
all eternity (Romans 6:23). God loved us all
so much that He gave His Son to take away
our sins. The gift of salvation is just that: a
gift. It is nothing you could ever earn. The
love of God is the greatest of all gifts, the
greatest of all blessings.

To love God is the greatest of virtues;
to be loved by God is the greatest of blessings.

And can it be that I should gain
An interest in the Savior's blood?
Died He for me, who caused His pain—
For me, who Him to death pursued?
Amazing love! How can it be,
That Thou, my God, shouldst die for me?

CHARLES WESLEY

True Love

Father, thank You for loving me enough to send
Your Son to take my place! I commit my heart
to You and ask You to be the Lord of my life.
Forgive my sins and show me how to live for You.
Thank You, Jesus, for Your sacrificial love for
me. Thank You for the example of true love
that You have provided. Amen.

The life of mortals is like grass, they flourish like a flower of the field; the wind blows over it and it is gone, and its place remembers it no more. But from everlasting to everlasting the LORD's love is with those who fear him, and his righteousness with their children's children—with those who keep his covenant and remember to obey his precepts.

PSALM 103:15–18 NIV

*All praise to God, the Father of our Lord Jesus Christ,
who has blessed us with every spiritual blessing in the
heavenly realms because we are united with Christ.
Even before he made the world, God loved us and chose
us in Christ to be holy and without fault in his eyes.*

EPHESIANS 1:3–4 NLT

Blue skies with white clouds on summer days.
A myriad of stars on clear moonlit nights.
Tulips and roses and violets and dandelions
and daisies. Bluebirds and laughter and
sunshine and Easter. See how He loves us!

ALICE CHAPIN

Abandon yourself utterly for the love of God,
and in this way you will become truly happy.

HENRY SUSO

Every single act of love bears the imprint of God.

UNKNOWN

Amazing Love

What amazing love You have blessed us with,
Father! A love I do not deserve. Let my heart be
filled with love for You so I can share this great
blessing with others. You are my hope in an often
hopeless world. You are my hope of heaven,
my hope of peace, my hope of change, purpose,
and unconditional love. Amen.

A rainbow stretches from one end of the sky to the other. Each shade of color, each facet of light, displays the radiant spectrum of God's love—a promise that He will always love each one of us at our worst and at our best.

UNKNOWN

May God send His love like sunshine in His warm and gentle way, to fill each corner of your heart each moment of today.

UNKNOWN

Love the LORD your God with all your heart and with all your soul and with all your strength. These commandments that I give you today are to be upon your hearts. Impress them on your children. Talk about them when you sit at home and when you walk along the road, when you lie down and when you get up. Tie them as symbols on your hands and bind them on your foreheads. Write them on the doorframes of your houses and on your gates.

DEUTERONOMY 6:5–9 NIV

But God demonstrates his own love for us in this:
While we were still sinners, Christ died for us.

ROMANS 5:8 NIV

How great is the goodness you have stored up for those
who fear you. You lavish it on those who come to you for
protection, blessing them before the watching world.
You hide them in the shelter of your presence, safe from
those who conspire against them. You shelter them in your
presence, far from accusing tongues. Praise the LORD,
for he has shown me the wonders of his unfailing love.

PSALM 31:19–21 NLT

A Wonderful Name

Jesus. What a wonderful name! It is the only name
we need to call upon for salvation. I praise You
for being the Way, the Truth, and the Life!
Thank You for calling me to be Your child.
I am so thankful that You love and care for me.
Help me to set my heart and mind on You, to be
an example of love for those around me. Amen.

God loves us, and the will of love
is always blessing for its loved ones.

HANNAH WHITALL SMITH

His overflowing love delights to make us
partakers of the bounties He graciously imparts.

HANNAH MOORE

The greatest honor we can give God is to live
gladly because of the knowledge of His love.

JULIAN OF NORWICH

He Keeps
His Promises

"The LORD himself goes before you and will be with you; he will never leave you nor forsake you. Do not be afraid; do not be discouraged."

DEUTERONOMY 31:8 NIV

Multiple times throughout the Bible, God promises He will never leave us nor forsake us. Christians throughout the ages will testify that God keeps His promises and that He is always with us. Even when it feels we are far from God or He doesn't see our circumstances, He is never far from any of us (Acts 17:27). When your faith is small and you have trouble trusting that God will do what He promised, look back on all the blessings you've claimed in your lifetime and ask the Lord to remind you of His faithfulness. He keeps His promises. When no one else in your life is worthy of your trust, you have a heavenly Father who can be counted on to do what He said He would do. People will let you down. Jesus never will. People will break promises. Jesus never will. The Lord is always with you, and you can trust Him!

LORD, you are mine! I promise to obey your words!
With all my heart I want your blessings. Be merciful
as you promised. I pondered the direction of my life,
and I turned to follow your laws.

PSALM 119:57–59 NLT

"Come to me, all you who are weary and burdened,
and I will give you rest. Take my yoke upon you and
learn from me, for I am gentle and humble in heart,
and you will find rest for your souls."

MATTHEW 11:28–29 NIV

Trusting in Your Promises

Father, You have promised to never leave
nor forsake me. Help me not to be afraid and to
trust in Your promises at all times. I know You
will never let me down. Thank You for Your
promise to guide me in all things great and small.
Your eye is always on me, keeping me from
error and ensuring that I can always find
a way home to You. Amen.

Glorious things of thee are spoken,
Zion, city of our God;
He, whose Word cannot be broken,
Formed thee for His own abode.

JOHN NEWTON

We may. . .depend upon God's promises,
for. . .He will be as good as His word.
He is so kind that He cannot deceive us,
so true that He cannot break His promise.

MATTHEW HENRY

Faith is two empty hands held
open to receive all of the Lord.

ALAN REDPATH

Love the LORD, all his faithful people!
The LORD preserves those who are true to him,
but the proud he pays back in full.
PSALM 31:23 NIV

"But blessed are those who trust in the LORD and
have made the LORD their hope and confidence."
JEREMIAH 17:7 NLT

*"And if I go and prepare a place for you,
I will come back and take you to be with
me that you also may be where I am."*

JOHN 14:3 NIV

*You prepare a feast for me in the presence of my enemies.
You honor me by anointing my head with oil. My cup
overflows with blessings. Surely your goodness and
unfailing love will pursue me all the days of my life,
and I will live in the house of the LORD forever.*

PSALM 23:5–6 NLT

My Life as Witness

Lord, I put my trust in You. I know You are good and You can be trusted. I believe Your promise to be faithful to me all the days of my life and You are going to prepare a place for me in heaven. Allow me to live my life with eternity in mind at all times. Let my life be a witness to all that You have done. Amen.

Standing on the promises of Christ the Lord,
Bound to Him eternally by love's strong cord,
Overcoming daily with the Spirit's sword,
Standing on the promises of God.

R. KELSO CARTER

God's blessings are dispersed according
to the riches of his grace, not according
to the depth of our faith.

MAX LUCADO

The LORD is a shelter for the oppressed, a refuge in times of
trouble. Those who know your name trust in you, for you,
O LORD, do not abandon those who search for you.
PSALM 9:9–10 NLT

The instructions of the LORD are perfect,
reviving the soul. The decrees of the LORD are
trustworthy, making wise the simple.
PSALM 19:7 NLT

Commit your way to the LORD, trust also
in Him, and He shall bring it to pass.
PSALM 37:5 NKJV

I have held many things in my hands,
and I have lost them all; but whatever I have
placed in God's hands, that I still possess.

MARTIN LUTHER

The beautiful thing about this adventure
called faith is that we can count on Him
never to lead us astray.

CHUCK SWINDOLL

You may trust in the Lord too little,
but you can never trust Him too much.

UNKNOWN

His Unfailing Love

I often feel that I lack faith, Lord—that You must be speaking promises for someone else, someone more faithful and deserving of them. Show me the error of this thinking. Thank You for Your unfailing love that pursues me each day, dear Lord! Amen.

"*Oh, that you would choose life, so that you and your descendants might live! You can make this choice by loving the LORD your God, obeying him, and committing yourself firmly to him. This is the key to your life. And if you love and obey the LORD, you will live long in the land the LORD swore to give your ancestors Abraham, Isaac, and Jacob.*"

DEUTERONOMY 30:19–20 NLT

Simple,
Everyday
Blessings

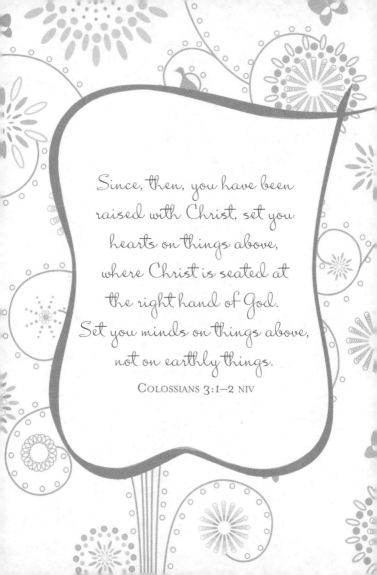

Since, then, you have been
raised with Christ, set you
hearts on things above,
where Christ is seated at
the right hand of God.
Set you minds on things above,
not on earthly things.

COLOSSIANS 3:1–2 NIV

We are often bombarded with troubles in this life: health issues, financial crisis, relation-ship problems, and many other daily trials that break our spirits. Jesus beckons us to focus on Him instead of worldly worries. Just as Peter walked on the water until he took his eyes off Christ and looked at the impossible mess he was in, so will we miss out on many of life's simple blessings when we look around at our own problems instead of setting our gaze on the Lord. God wants to bless us in the midst of the mess of life. Daily He sends little reminders that He is with us and watching over us. Take a look around you and thank God for all of the simple blessings we often take for granted. If our hearts are set on things above, we'll never miss the simple, everyday blessings God sends our way.

I thank God for all things good—peace,
happiness, laughter, and friends.

BONNIE JENSEN

The heart is rich when it is content, and it is
always content when its desires are fixed on God.

MIGUEL FEBRES CORDERO-MUÑOZ

The Center of My Day

When I set my mind on You, heavenly Father,
I'm much more aware of the simple and
many ways You bless me every day. Be the
center of my day so that I don't miss out on
what You want to show me. I don't want to dwell
on what might happen in the future; I want to
relish this chance to nurture and cherish the
blessings You've given me. Amen

Look upon the skies, the earth, and the air as
celestial joys. . .as if you were among the angels.

THOMAS TRAHERNE

God writes the gospel not in the Bible alone,
but on trees and flowers and clouds and stars.

MARTIN LUTHER

Your only treasures are those
which you carry in your heart.

DEMOPHILUS

Blessed is the one who does not walk in step with the wicked or stand in the way that sinners take or sit in the company of mockers, but whose delight is in the law of the LORD, and who meditates on his law day and night. That person is like a tree planted by streams of water, which yields its fruit in season and whose leaf does not wither—whatever they do prospers.

PSALM 1:1–3 NIV

How joyful are those who fear the LORD—all who follow
his ways! You will enjoy the fruit of your labor.
How joyful and prosperous you will be!
PSALM 128:1–2 NLT

Blessings crown the head of the righteous,
but violence overwhelms the mouth of the wicked.
PROVERBS 10:6 NIV

A Cheerful Worker

Heavenly Father, thank You for the work You've given me to do. I choose to honor You in my life, my work, and in everything I do. I want to please You in every little detail of my life. Sometimes I need an attitude adjustment that can only come from You. Let me be a cheerful worker. Amen.

All that is good, all that is true, all that
is beautiful, all that is beneficent, be it
great or small, be it perfect or fragmentary,
natural as well as supernatural, moral as
well as material, comes from God.

John Newman

Nothing is worth more than today.

Johann Wolfgang von Goethe

Happy is the man who finds wisdom, and the man who gains understanding; for her proceeds are better than the profits of silver, and her gain than fine gold.

PROVERBS 3:13–14 NKJV

"The LORD bless you and keep you; the LORD make His face shine on you, and be gracious to you; the LORD lift up His countenance on you, and give you peace."

NUMBERS 6:24–26 NASB

The sun. . .in its full glory, either at rising
or setting—this and many other like blessings we
enjoy daily; and for the most of them, because
they are so common, most men forget to
pay their praises. But let us not.

IZAAK WALTON

Let there be many windows in your soul,
that all the glory of the universe may beautify it.

ELLA WHEELER WILCOX

God's in His heaven—all's right with the world.

ROBERT BROWNING

An Eternal
Reward

For I am convinced that neither death nor life, neither angels nor demons, neither the present nor the future, nor any powers, neither height nor depth, nor anything else in all creation, will be able to separate us from the love of God that is in Christ Jesus our Lord.

ROMANS 8:38–39 NIV

God's Word tells us that He has set eternity in our hearts (Ecclesiastes 3:11). It is something we long for all the days of our earthly life. God went to great lengths to make sure we could inherit His blessing of love and eternal life. He sent His Son, Jesus, to exhibit His love and make a way for us to be with Him for all eternity. He reminds us that nothing—absolutely nothing—can separate us from His love. That's our eternal reward, to live unseparated from God's love for all eternity! And we don't have to wait until heaven to receive *that* blessing. He offers His love to us right now. We just need to accept it and live in it as we look forward to eternity. Are you living in God's love? Ask the Lord to show you the truth of His love today. The rewards are eternal.

I would not give one moment of heaven for all
the joys and riches of the world, even if it lasted
for thousands and thousands of years.

MARTIN LUTHER

Nothing can separate you from His love,
absolutely nothing. . . . God is enough for time,
and God is enough for eternity. God is enough!

HANNAH WHITALL SMITH

Don't put your confidence in powerful people;
there is no help for you there. When they breathe their last,
they return to the earth, and all their plans die with
them. But joyful are those who have the God of Israel
as their helper, whose hope is in the LORD their God.
He made heaven and earth, the sea, and everything in
them. He keeps every promise forever.

PSALM 146:3–6 NLT

You have set Your glory above the heavens.
Thy glory flames from sun and star:
Center and soul of every sphere,
Yet to each loving heart how near.

OLIVER WENDELL HOLMES

From faith to faith, from grace to grace,
So in Thy strength shall I go on,
Till heaven and earth flee from Thy face,
And glory end what grace begun.

WOLFGANG DESSLER

A Heavenly Reward

Lord, You have promised my eternal award.
I know that no matter how much I do here on
earth that gets unnoticed by others, You notice.
I know my reward is in heaven with You. I will
do my best, not to be seen by those around me,
but to honor You. Amen.

"Repent, then, and turn to God, so that your sins may be wiped out, that times of refreshing may come from the Lord, and that he may send the Messiah, who has been appointed for you—even Jesus."
ACTS 3:19–20 NIV

He has made everything beautiful in its time. He has also set eternity in the human heart; yet no one can fathom what God has done from beginning to end.
ECCLESIASTES 3:11 NIV

Turn us again to yourself, O God. Make your face shine down upon us. Only then will we be saved.
PSALM 80:3 NLT

LORD, you alone are my inheritance, my cup of blessing. You guard all that is mine. The land you have given me is a pleasant land. What a wonderful inheritance!

PSALM 16:5–6 NLT

All praise to God, the Father of our Lord Jesus Christ, who has blessed us with every spiritual blessing in the heavenly realms because we are united with Christ.

EPHESIANS 1:3 NLT

Aim at heaven and you will get earth thrown in.
Aim at earth and you get neither.

C. S. LEWIS

God hath given to man a short time
here upon earth, and yet upon this
short time eternity depends.

JEREMY TAYLOR

Longing for Heaven

Heavenly Father, some days I long for heaven.
This world is difficult and troubling. Help me
to keep plugging away knowing that one day
we'll meet face-to-face and my tears will be
wiped away by Your loving hands. Amen.

The smallest bits of obedience opens
heaven, and the deepest truths of God
immediately become ours.

OSWALD CHAMBERS

When the soul has laid down its faults at the feet
of God, it feels as though it had wings.

EUGENIE DE GUERIN

When morning gilds the skies,
my heart awakening cries:
May Jesus Christ be praised!

JOSEPH BARNBY

Sing to the Lord, bless His name; proclaim the
good news of His salvation from day to day.
PSALM 96:2 NKJV

"Only in returning to me and resting in me will you be
saved. In quietness and confidence is your strength."
ISAIAH 30:15 NLT

Our earthly bodies are planted in the ground when we die,
but they will be raised to live forever.
1 CORINTHIANS 15:42 NLT

Life is eternal, and love is immortal,
and death is only a horizon; and a horizon
is nothing save the limit of our sight.

ROSSITER WORTHINGTON RAYMOND

May your life become one of glad and unending
praise to the Lord as you journey through this
world, and in the world that is to come!

TERESA OF AVILA

Faith is to believe what we do not see; and the
reward of this faith is to see what we believe.

ST. AUGUSTINE

Blessed Freedom
in Christ

It is for freedom that
Christ has set us free.
Stand firm, then, and do
not let yourselves be burdened
again by a yoke of slavery.

GALATIANS 5:1 NIV

Freedom in Christ is more than just being free
from sin and securing our place in heaven.
Freedom in Christ means that we can be free
here and now—to live a life of purpose, to
hope, and to dream. We don't have to be
imprisoned by negative thinking or worried
about what others think of us. We don't have
to watch our backs or concern ourselves
over idle gossip. Freedom in Christ gives us
confidence to be all that God made us to be.
We are no longer held captive by fear! The
perfect love Christ offers us casts out all fear
(1 John 4:18), and we can have true peace—a
peace that transcends all understanding—here
on earth while we live our daily lives. When
we live like we're free in Christ, our insecurities fade, our fears diminish, and love takes
over.

Those who run in the path of God's commands
have their hearts set free.
JOANIE GARBORG

You cast my fear away and loved
me perfectly I am free
Free to hope like my life isn't worthless
Dream like my future has purpose
Live like I'm free and I am yours.
MARILEE PARRISH "LIVE LIKE I'M FREE"

What can I offer the LORD for all he has done for me?
I will lift up the cup of salvation and praise the LORD's
name for saving me. I will keep my promises to the LORD
in the presence of all his people. The LORD cares deeply
when his loved ones die. O LORD, I am your servant;
yes, I am your servant, born into your household.

PSALM 116:12–16 NLT

From God, great and small, rich and poor,
draw living water from a living spring,
and those who serve Him freely and gladly
will receive grace answering to grace.

THOMAS À KEMPIS

God wants nothing from us except our needs,
and these furnish Him with room to display
His bounty when He supplies them freely. . . .
Not what I have, but what I do not have, is the
first point of contact between my soul and God.

CHARLES H. SPURGEON

Real Freedom

Father, thank You for the freedom you've given
me in Christ! Freedom to live for You, to dream,
to hope, and to live a life of meaning. You have
freed me from death. You have freed me from
my enemies. I praise You and worship you
for all You have done! Amen.

"The LORD lives! Praise be to my Rock!
Exalted be my God, the Rock, my Savior!
He is the God who avenges me, who puts the
nations under me, who sets me free from my enemies."
2 SAMUEL 22:47–49 NIV

In my distress I prayed to the LORD, and the LORD answered
me and set me free. The LORD is for me, so I will have
no fear. What can mere people do to me?
PSALM 118:5–6 NLT

New hopes come crowding on
the man who is saved by grace.

CHARLES H. SPURGEON

I hear it in the twilight still, and at the
sunset hour—I'm saved by grace! What words
can thrill with such a magic power?

FANNY CROSBY

Like any other gift, the gift of grace can be yours
only if you'll reach out and take it. Maybe being
able to reach out and take it is a gift, too.

FREDERICK BUECHNER

Love flies, runs, and rejoices;
it is free and nothing can hold it back.

THOMAS À KEMPIS

Fountain of grace, rich, full and free,
What need I, that is not in Thee?
Full pardon, strength to meet the day,
And peace which none can take away.

JAMES EDMESTON

Nothing to Fear

Set me free, Lord, set me free! Sometimes
I live captive by my own thoughts and fears.
But I trust that You can help me overcome
my insecurities and live with my heart set on
You. Father, help me to get over self-doubt.
Remind me that Your blessings are forever
and I have nothing to fear. Amen.

*Now God's wonderful grace rules instead,
giving us right standing with God and resulting
in eternal life through Jesus Christ our Lord.*

ROMANS 5:21 NLT

*Therefore, since we have been justified through faith, we
have peace with God through our Lord Jesus Christ, through
whom we have gained access by faith into this grace in which
we now stand. And we boast in the hope of the glory of God.*

ROMANS 5:1–2 NIV

He's in Control

"The God who made the world and everything in it is the Lord of heaven and earth and does not live in temples built by human hands. And he is not served by human hands, as if he needed anything. Rather, he himself gives everyone life and breath and everything else."

ACTS 17: 24–25 NIV

Isn't it amazing that the God who formed the earth and established it upon the waters is the same God who knows us intimately and wants a very personal relationship with us? God's Word tells us He knows when we sit down and stand up. He knows our words before we speak them! (Psalm 139). God had already determined where and when we should live, long before we were ever born. What a comfort to know He's in control! He knows everything that has happened and will happen to us. He is not far from any of us! Everything that comes our way has passed through His hands first. We are safe in His arms.

"From one man he made all the nations, that they should inhabit the whole earth; and he marked out their appointed times in history and the boundaries of their lands. God did this so that they would seek him and perhaps reach out for him and find him, though he is not far from any one of us."

ACTS 17: 26–27 NIV

What an astonishment it will be to find, when the
veil is lifted, the souls that have been reaped by
you, simply because you had been in the habit
of taking your orders from Jesus Christ.

OSWALD CHAMBERS

Only God gives true peace—a quiet gift
He sets within us just when we think
we've exhausted our search for it.

UNKNOWN

God is as great in minuteness
as He is in magnitude.

UNKNOWN

And God will generously provide all you need.
Then you will always have everything you need
and plenty left over to share with others.

2 CORINTHIANS 9:8 NLT

The LORD is the strength of his people,
a fortress of salvation for his anointed one.
Save your people and bless your inheritance;
be their shepherd and carry them forever.

PSALM 28:8–9 NIV

Your Plan Is Best

Dear Lord, what a comfort to know that You see my circumstances and that You are in control! I'm often tempted to handle things in my own way, but I'm learning that Your plan is always best. I will put my trust in You. Amen.

If you want to make God laugh,
tell Him about your plans.

WOODY ALLEN

Speak to Him often of your business,
your plans, your troubles, your fears—
of everything that concerns you.

ALPHONSUS LIGUORI

Always be in a state of expectancy, and see that
you leave room for God to come in as He likes.

OSWALD CHAMBERS

For those with faith, no explanation is necessary.
For those without, no explanation is possible.

THOMAS AQUINAS

Before me, even as behind,
God is, and all is well.

JOHN GREENLEAF WHITTIER

The God who holds the whole world in His
hands wraps Himself in the splendor of the
sun's light and walks among the clouds.

UNKNOWN

*"But when he, the Spirit of truth, comes,
he will guide you into all the truth. He will not
speak on his own; he will speak only what he hears,
and he will tell you what is yet to come."*

JOHN 16:13 NIV

*"The LORD will guide you always; he will satisfy
your needs in a sun-scorched land and will strengthen
your frame. You will be like a well-watered garden,
like a spring whose waters never fail."*

ISAIAH 58:11 NIV

My Life Is in Your Hands

Father God, how amazing it is to me that
You are the creator of the universe—
You're the One who placed the stars in the sky—
and yet You care for me deeply! When I put
my life in Your hands, I am safe. Amen.

When you have. . .accomplished your daily task,
go to sleep in peace. God is awake.
VICTOR HUGO

I avoid looking forward or backward,
and try to keep looking upward.
CHARLOTTE BRONTË

We benefit eternally by God's
being just what He is.
UNKNOWN

Comfort for Today

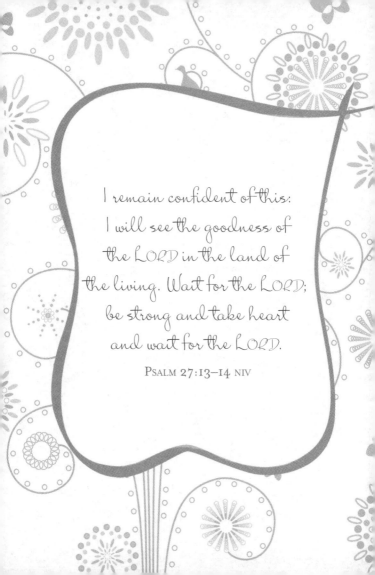

I remain confident of this:
I will see the goodness of
the LORD in the land of
the living. Wait for the LORD;
be strong and take heart
and wait for the LORD.

PSALM 27:13–14 NIV

God never changes. He sees His people through hard times. God is good and He is working everything that happens in your life for *your* good (Romans 8:28). Be comforted today knowing if we wait on the Lord and trust in His purpose and timing, we will see His goodness in this life. If we cast our burdens and cares on Him, He will sustain us and won't let us fall (Psalm 55:22). Know that God sees your situation and your circumstances. He loves you and He cares. Trust that He is working in your life, behind the scenes, orchestrating a grand finale that you can't hear or see just yet. Ask for His guidance and seek His face today as you wait on Him. And be on the lookout for the miracles and blessings—big and small—that God is sending your way.

Strength for today and bright hope for tomorrow,
Blessings all mine, with ten thousand beside!

THOMAS O. CHISHOLM

From the simple seeds of childlike faith,
we reap the lovely harvest of God's
reassuring presence in our lives.

UNKNOWN

Let the matchless love of God sweep away
your doubts and fears. You already have
God's attention, and you will never lose it.

JONI EARECKSON TADA

*Though I am surrounded by troubles, you will protect me
from the anger of my enemies. You reach out your hand,
and the power of your right hand saves me. The LORD will
work out his plans for my life—for your faithful love,
O LORD, endures forever. Don't abandon me, for you made me.*
PSALM 138:7–8 NLT

Comfort is not the absence of problems;
comfort is the strength to face my problems.
KEN HUTCHERSON

Amazing grace! How sweet the sound
That saved a wretch like me!
I once was lost, but now am found;
Was blind, but now I see.
JOHN NEWTON

We have a God who delights in impossibilities.
ANDREW MURRAY

No Worries

Lord, help me not to borrow trouble by
worrying about tomorrow. Thank You for
giving me strength and comfort for each day.
As long as I trust in Your presence, I have
nothing to worry about. Nothing can separate
me from You, because You are the strong
protector, the mighty One who watches
over me always. Amen.

God didn't promise days without pain,
laughter without sorrow, sun without rain,
but He did promise strength for the day,
comfort for the tears, and light for the way.

UNKNOWN

Jesus, Thou art all compassion,
Pure unbounded love Thou art;
Visit us with Thy salvation;
Enter every trembling heart.

CHARLES WESLEY

We shall find peace. We shall hear the angels,
we shall see the sky sparkling with diamonds.

ANTON CHEKHOV

The Lord gives strength to his people;
the Lord blesses his people with peace.

PSALM 29:11 NIV

Praise be to the God and Father of our Lord Jesus Christ,
the Father of compassion and the God of all comfort.

2 CORINTHIANS 1:3 NIV

The Lord is a refuge for the oppressed, a stronghold in
times of trouble. Those who know your name trust in you,
for you, Lord, have never forsaken those who seek you.

PSALM 9:9–10 NIV

*Therefore we have been comforted in your comfort.
And we rejoiced exceedingly more for the joy of Titus,
because his spirit has been refreshed by you all.*

2 CORINTHIANS 7:13 NKJV

*Shout for joy, you heavens; rejoice, you earth;
burst into song, you mountains! For the LORD comforts his
people and will have compassion on his afflicted ones.*

ISAIAH 49:13 NIV

I Am Loved

Father, when troubles come, I never have to face them alone. You are my refuge and strength. You comfort me in times of trouble, and You watch over me from day to day. I tell You my problems and You listen, Lord. I speak of the good things in my life and You smile. I ask You for advice, knowing it will come in Your time. I am no longer lonely; I am loved. Amen.

Contentment is not the fulfillment
of what you want, but the realization
of how much you already have.

UNKNOWN

Where the soul is full of peace and joy,
outward surroundings and circumstances
are of comparatively little account.

HANNAH WHITALL SMITH

The soul is a temple, and God is silently
building it by night and by day. Precious thoughts
are building it, unselfish love is building it;
all-penetrating faith is building it.

HENRY WARD BEECHER

Cultivating a
Thankful Heart

I will praise you, LORD,
with all my heart; before the
"gods" I will sing your praise.
I will bow down toward your
holy temple and will praise
your name for your unfailing
love and your faithfulness,
for you have so exalted your
solemn decree that it surpasses
your fame.

PSALM 138:1–2 NIV

Start your morning by thanking God for a new day, knowing that His mercies and compassion are new every morning (Lamentations 3:22–23). Keep a song of praise in your heart throughout the day, thanking God for His many blessings. Thank Him for the simple things in life: meals, friends, family, smiles from children, a roof over your head, a warm place to sleep, clothing, and transportation. Say "Thank You!" *out loud* to God. Tell Him how thankful you are for His love, for His Son, for His gift of life now and for eternity. In the evening, thank Him for family time, for a job that provides, for a freshly prepared dinner. As you rest your head on your pillow, thank God for a full day, for the little blessings you witnessed throughout the day, for how He was with you through it all, and will be again tomorrow and for all eternity. *That's* how you cultivate a thankful heart.

Seeing our Father in everything makes life one
long thanksgiving and gives a rest of heart.
HANNAH WHITALL SMITH

If anyone would tell you the shortest, surest
way to happiness and all perfection, he must
tell you to make it a rule to thank and praise
God for everything that happens to you.
WILLIAM LAW

*May God be merciful and bless us. May his face smile
with favor on us. . . . May your ways be known
throughout the earth, your saving power among people
everywhere. May the nations praise you,
O God. Yes, may all the nations praise you.*

PSALM 67:1–3 NLT

*This service that you perform is not only supplying
the needs of the Lord's people but is also overflowing
in many expressions of thanks to God.*

2 CORINTHIANS 9:12 NIV

Thou who hast given so much to me,
give one more thing—a grateful heart.
GEORGE HERBERT

Cherish all your happy moments;
they make a fine cushion for old age.
BOOTH TARKINGTON

The private and personal blessings we enjoy
deserve the thanksgiving of a whole life.
JEREMY TAYLOR

A Thankful Heart

Create a thankful heart in me, Father. I need
Your gentle wisdom for every area of my life.
I'm so thankful that what You offer is the best.
Thank You for my family. Thank You for my
friends. Thank You for always providing for me.
Thank You! Amen.

To be thankful for all is to
accept grace to its fullest.

UNKNOWN

Were there no God, we would be in this glorious
world with grateful hearts and no one to thank.

CHRISTINA ROSSETTI

*Since we are receiving a Kingdom that is unshakable,
let us be thankful and please God by worshiping
him with holy fear and awe.*

HEBREWS 12:28 NLT

*Devote yourselves to prayer with
an alert mind and a thankful heart.*

COLOSSIANS 4:2 NLT

*Let the peace of Christ rule in your hearts,
since as members of one body you were
called to peace. And be thankful.*

COLOSSIANS 3:15 NIV

I urge, then, first of all, that petitions, prayers, intercession and thanksgiving be made for all people—for kings and all those in authority, that we may live peaceful and quiet lives in all godliness and holiness. This is good, and pleases God our Savior, who wants all people to be saved and to come to a knowledge of the truth.

1 TIMOTHY 2:1–4 NIV

Worship the LORD with gladness. Come before him, singing with joy.

PSALM 100:2 NLT

Always Thankful

Heavenly Father, let the peace of Christ
take control of my heart so that I can be
thankful at all times. Even when I'm having
trouble finding things for which to be thankful.
Help me to remember that You have always
been faithful to me. Amen.

For health and food, for love of friends,
for everything Thy goodness sends,
Father in heaven, we thank Thee.
RALPH WALDO EMERSON

There is always something
for which to be thankful.
CHARLES DICKENS

Be thankful for the least gift,
so shalt thou be meant to receive greater.
THOMAS À KEMPIS

Being a Blessing
to Others

"Give, and it will be given to you. A good measure, pressed down, shaken together and running over, will be poured into your lap. For with the measure you use, it will be measured to you."

LUKE 6:38 NIV

When we give of ourselves without seeking our own glory, God will bless that abundantly! There is so much joy in forgetting yourself and knowing that someone else is being blessed by what you've done. Sometimes our good deeds go unnoticed by people, but don't let this stop you. Let others see Christ shining through you! Ask God to show you how you might bless another person *without* getting noticed today. If we're doing everything for the glory of God, it won't matter if others take notice or not. But if they do notice our good deeds, our hope is that they will praise God and see His love through what we've done. And don't forget to give back to God what He's given you by tithing. He promises to bless you when you do so (Malachi 3:10). If all Christians gave back their tithe as God has asked, there would be enough food and supplies for everyone in need.

*"Bring all the tithes into the storehouse so there will be enough food in my Temple. If you do," says the L*ORD* of Heaven's Armies, "I will open the windows of heaven for you. I will pour out a blessing so great you won't have enough room to take it in! Try it! Put me to the test!"*

MALACHI 3:10 NLT

A kind heart is a fountain of gladness, making everything in its vicinity freshen into smiles.
WASHINGTON IRVING

We were not sent into this world to do anything into which we cannot put our heart.
JOHN RUSKIN

We are to turn our back upon evil, and in every way possible, do good, help people, and bring blessings into their lives.
NORMAN VINCENT PEALE

Happiness is a perfume you cannot pour on others
without getting a few drops on yourself.

RALPH WALDO EMERSON

Your greatest pleasure is that which rebounds
from hearts that you have made glad.

HENRY WARD BEECHER

The lives that have been the greatest blessing to you
are the lives of those people who themselves were
unaware of having been a blessing.

OSWALD CHAMBERS

Serving Others

Father, help me put my whole heart into
serving You and blessing others. I want to be a
giver. Put people into my life that I can bless.
Teach me to serve, to love, to be honest,
to put the needs of others first—to live a humble
but blessed life. Show me how I can best serve
others for the glory of Your name. Amen.

Those who live only to satisfy their own sinful nature will harvest decay and death from that sinful nature. But those who live to please the Spirit will harvest everlasting life from the Spirit. So let's not get tired of doing what is good. At just the right time we will reap a harvest of blessing if we don't give up. Therefore, whenever we have the opportunity, we should do good to everyone— especially to those in the family of faith.

GALATIANS 6:8–10 NLT

Then Jesus said to his host, "When you give a luncheon or dinner, do not invite your friends, your brothers or sisters, your relatives, or your rich neighbors; if you do, they may invite you back and so you will be repaid. But when you give a banquet, invite the poor, the crippled, the lame, the blind, and you will be blessed. Although they cannot repay you, you will be repaid at the resurrection of the righteous."

LUKE 14:12–14 NIV

Use what talent you possess—the woods
would be very silent if no birds sang
except those that sang best.

HENRY VAN DYKE

Every heart that has beat strong and cheerfully has
left a hopeful impulse behind it in the world and
bettered the tradition of mankind.

ROBERT LOUIS STEVENSON

If we learn how to give of ourselves, to forgive
others, and to live with thanksgiving,
we need not seek happiness. It will seek us.

UNKNOWN

Doing What's Right

Dear Lord, help me to never get tired of doing what is right. Sustain me when I feel like giving up. Your Word promises a harvest of blessing for doing the right thing, and I trust You to keep that promise. Whenever I feel pressure to exalt myself above others, Lord, remind me that my worth is found in You alone. Amen.

Finally, all of you should be of one mind. Sympathize with each other. Love each other as brothers and sisters. Be tenderhearted, and keep a humble attitude. Don't repay evil for evil. Don't retaliate with insults when people insult you. Instead, pay them back with a blessing. That is what God has called you to do, and he will bless you for it.

1 PETER 3:8–9 NLT

And It Will Surprise You What the Lord Has Done

But let all who take refuge in you be glad; let them ever sing for joy. Spread your protection over them, that those who love your name may rejoice in you. Surely, LORD, you bless the righteous; you surround them with your favor as with a shield.

PSALM 5:11–12 NIV

Have you sat down and counted your blessings? Have you written them down? It's so important to journal God's miracles and blessings in your life so you can see all that the Lord has done for you. Take the time to count and record your blessings. Write them in a journal, start a blog, create a blessing scrapbook—whatever works best for you. And keep it handy! Remember that hard times will come your way. That's a guarantee in this old world. But won't it be great to pull out your chronicle of God's blessings in your own life in the midst of your trials? Not only will that help you get your mind off your temporary troubles, you can worship and praise God as you recount the ways He has been faithful to you in the past. What a blessing!

*But the wisdom from above is first of all pure. It is
also peace loving, gentle at all times, and willing to
yield to others. It is full of mercy and good deeds.
It shows no favoritism and is always sincere.*

JAMES 3:17 NLT

*We count as blessed those who have persevered.
You have heard of Job's perseverance and have
seen what the Lord finally brought about.
The Lord is full of compassion and mercy.*

JAMES 5:11 NIV

He Is Generous

Father, You have given us Your Word and Your Holy Spirit to teach us. And You give wisdom to all of us generously, just by asking! I pray that You would grant that request and fill me with the mercy and blessings of living a holy life. Amen.

Riches take wings, comforts vanish,
hope withers away, but love stays with us.
God is love.

LEW WALLACE

Every person's life is a fairy
tale written by God's fingers.

HANS CHRISTIAN ANDERSEN

There is nothing but God's grace. We walk upon
it; we breathe it; we live and die by it; it makes
the nails and axles of the universe.

ROBERT LOUIS STEVENSON

Be on the lookout for mercies. The more we look for them, the more of them we will see. Blessings brighten when we count them.

MALTBIE D. BABCOCK

You never can measure what God will do through you. . . . Keep your relationship right with Him, then whatever circumstances you are in, and whoever you meet day by day, He is pouring rivers of living water through you.

OSWALD CHAMBERS

*Through Christ Jesus, God has blessed the Gentiles
with the same blessing he promised to Abraham,
so that we who are believers might receive
the promised Holy Spirit through faith.*

GALATIANS 3:14 NLT

*"All who are victorious will inherit all these blessings,
and I will be their God, and they will be my children."*

REVELATION 21:7 NLT

Your Gentle Strength

Father God, though Your strength is limitless,
it's tempered with wisdom and gentleness.
You are both my strong tower and my tender,
loving Father. You have given me everything!
You have blessed me beyond my imagination
and have called me Your child.